Unveiling the Tapestry: The Effects of European Colonialism on African National Borders

Copyright Page

TITLE: Unveiling the Tapestry: The Effects of European Colonialism on African National Boundaries

1ST Edition

Copyright @ 2023

Roberto M. Rodriguez. All rights reserved.

ISBN: 9798223358879

Table of Contents

Unveiling the Tapestry: The Effects of European Colonialism on African National Borders

By Roberto Miguel Rodriguez

Chapter 1: The Effects of European Colonialism on African National Borders

The Historical Context of European Colonialism in Africa

European colonialism in Africa had a profound and lasting impact on the continent, shaping its national borders and influencing various aspects of African societies. Understanding the historical context of this colonial period is crucial to comprehending the effects it had on African nations and ethnic groups.

During the late 19th and early 20th centuries, European powers, including Britain, France, Germany, Belgium, Portugal, and Italy, embarked on a race to colonize Africa. This scramble for Africa was driven by economic, political, and strategic motives. The industrial revolution in Europe created a demand for raw materials, and Africa was seen as an abundant source. Additionally, the desire to establish colonies as outlets for surplus population and to gain prestige fueled this expansion.

The partitioning of Africa was accomplished through a series of conferences, most notably the Berlin Conference of 1884-1885, where European powers carved up the continent with little regard for its existing ethnic, linguistic, and cultural boundaries. This artificial division resulted in the creation of national borders that often cut across ethnic groups, leading to long-lasting tensions and conflicts.

The economic impacts of European colonialism on African nations were significant. The colonizers exploited Africa's resources, such as minerals, timber, and agricultural products, for their own benefit, resulting in economic underdevelopment and dependence for the African countries. The introduction of cash-crop agriculture disrupted traditional subsistence practices and led to a decline in food security.

Colonial rule also had social and cultural consequences in post-colonial Africa. The imposition of European educational systems and languages eroded indigenous knowledge and languages, creating educational disparities and inequalities. The introduction of Western cultural norms and values also challenged traditional African social structures and identities.

Politically, European colonialism exacerbated existing ethnic divisions and created power struggles among different groups. The arbitrary drawing of borders and the favoritism shown towards certain ethnic groups by the colonizers led to ethnic conflicts and tensions that continue to plague many African countries today.

The environmental consequences of European colonialism were also severe. The extraction of natural resources and the introduction of cash-crop agriculture contributed to deforestation, soil erosion, and the degradation of ecosystems. This has had long-term impacts on the environment, including the loss of biodiversity and increased vulnerability to climate change.

Furthermore, the partitioning of ethnic groups resulting from colonial borders had significant human rights implications. Forced displacement and relocation of populations led to the violation of basic rights and the loss of ancestral lands. Ethnic minorities often faced discrimination and marginalization in the newly created nations.

The legacy of European colonialism in Africa is still visible today, with ongoing struggles for self-determination and the resolution of ethnic conflicts. Understanding this historical context is essential for historians to grasp the multifaceted effects of European colonialism on African national borders, ethnic groups, economies, societies, politics, environment, human rights, and healthcare. Only by unraveling this complex tapestry can we gain insights into the challenges and opportunities faced by African nations in the post-colonial era.

The Creation of National Borders in Africa

Introduction:

The creation of national borders in Africa during the era of European colonialism has had profound and lasting effects on the continent. This subchapter aims to delve into the multifaceted consequences of this historical event on various aspects of African societies. From economic and political impacts to social and cultural consequences, this chapter seeks to provide a comprehensive analysis of the effects of European colonialism on African national borders.

The Partition of Ethnic Groups:

One of the most significant outcomes of the creation of national borders in Africa was the arbitrary division of ethnic groups. European colonizers paid little heed to the complex ethnic dynamics and cultural landscapes of the continent, resulting in the partitioning of ethnic communities across multiple countries. This subchapter explores the long-lasting impact of this partition on the identity, self-determination struggles, and ethnic conflicts that emerged as a consequence.

Economic Impacts of European Colonialism:

European colonialism in Africa had far-reaching economic implications. The arbitrary borders drawn by colonizers disrupted preexisting trade networks and hindered the development of a cohesive regional economy. This section analyzes the economic consequences of colonialism, including resource extraction, exploitative labor practices, and the perpetuation of economic inequalities that persist to this day.

Social and Cultural Consequences of National Borders:

The imposition of national borders in Africa also had profound social and cultural effects. This subchapter investigates the challenges faced by ethnic communities in maintaining their cultural heritage and traditions in the face of border restrictions. It also explores the impact on educational disparities, health and healthcare challenges, and the displacement of ethnic populations due to migration patterns resulting from colonial borders.

Political Effects of European Colonialism:

European colonialism significantly shaped the political landscape of Africa. This section delves into the legacy of colonial borders on governance structures, including the emergence of post-colonial nation-states and the challenges faced in maintaining political stability. It also examines the human rights issues resulting from the partitioning of ethnic groups and the implications for democratic processes and political participation.

Environmental Consequences of European Colonialism:

The creation of national borders in Africa also had environmental repercussions. This subchapter explores the impact of colonialism on land degradation, natural resource exploitation, and the disruption of ecological systems. It highlights the need for sustainable environmental practices and international cooperation to address these challenges.

Conclusion:

The creation of national borders in Africa during European colonialism has had far-reaching consequences across various dimensions of African societies. From economic disparities and political instability to social and cultural disruptions, the effects of colonialism continue to shape the continent. By understanding these historical legacies, policymakers and scholars can work towards addressing the challenges and promoting a more equitable and sustainable future for Africa.

The Role of European Powers in Partitioning Ethnic Groups

European colonialism in Africa had a profound impact on the national borders and the partitioning of ethnic groups on the continent. This subchapter explores the role that European powers played in this process, shedding light on the historical events that led to the creation of national borders and the subsequent consequences for ethnic groups in Africa.

During the late 19th and early 20th centuries, European powers, primarily Britain, France, Belgium, Germany, and Portugal, embarked on a scramble for Africa, dividing the continent amongst themselves. The Berlin Conference of 1884-1885 formalized this colonization, with European powers carving out territories without considering the ethnic, linguistic, or cultural makeup of the African peoples living there.

The partitioning of ethnic groups had severe implications for the people of Africa. Many ethnic communities found themselves arbitrarily divided by the newly drawn borders, leading to the fragmentation of tribes, families, and communities. Traditional lands, which held deep cultural and spiritual significance, were split between different colonial territories.

Furthermore, European powers often favored certain ethnic groups over others, exacerbating existing ethnic tensions and deepening divisions. This manipulation of ethnic groups for colonial interests fueled conflicts and rivalries that continue to be felt in post-colonial Africa.

The economic impacts of this partitioning were substantial. Natural resources and trade routes were exploited by the European colonizers, often leaving African nations economically dependent and disadvantaged. The national borders created by European powers disrupted longstanding trade networks and hindered economic cooperation between ethnic groups.

Socially and culturally, the consequences of national borders in post-colonial Africa were profound. Traditional ways of life were disrupted, as communities were forced to adapt to new political boundaries. Cultural practices and languages were suppressed, as European powers imposed their own languages and systems of governance.

Politically, the partitioning of ethnic groups had lasting effects. European powers established colonial administrations that favored certain ethnic groups, leading to political inequalities and power imbalances. These divisions, often based on ethnic identity, continue to shape political dynamics in many African nations today.

The environmental consequences of European colonialism and national borders were also significant. Traditional land management practices that had sustained ecosystems for generations were disrupted, leading to deforestation, soil degradation, and loss of biodiversity.

Human rights issues arose as a result of the partitioning of ethnic groups in Africa. Forced displacement, violence, and the denial of basic rights to certain groups became common occurrences. The consequences of these violations continue to be felt today, as marginalized communities struggle for recognition and justice.

In terms of education and healthcare, the partitioning of ethnic groups resulted in disparities and inequalities. Access to quality education and healthcare services varied greatly depending on the ethnic group and the colonial power in control of the territory.

Migration patterns and displacement of ethnic populations were also a direct consequence of the colonial borders. Many ethnic groups found themselves on the wrong side of the divide, leading to forced migrations and the displacement of communities from their ancestral lands.

The struggle for identity and self-determination among ethnic groups affected by European colonialism in Africa continues to this day. Many communities face challenges in asserting their cultural identity and exercising their right to self-governance within the confines of national borders imposed by colonial powers.

In conclusion, the role of European powers in partitioning ethnic groups in Africa had far-reaching consequences. The arbitrary drawing of national borders disrupted social, cultural, economic, and political dynamics, leading to ongoing challenges and conflicts. Understanding this historical context is crucial for comprehending the complexities of post-colonial Africa and addressing the issues faced by ethnic groups in the region.

Chapter 2: Economic Impacts of European Colonialism on African Nations

Exploitation of Natural Resources by European Colonizers

European colonization of Africa had far-reaching effects on the continent's natural resources. This subchapter explores the impact of European colonialism on the exploitation of Africa's rich resources, shedding light on the environmental, economic, and social consequences that persist to this day.

The arrival of European colonizers in Africa marked the beginning of an era of resource exploitation. Natural resources, such as minerals, timber, and agricultural products, were viewed as valuable commodities and were ruthlessly extracted by the colonizers for their own economic gain. This relentless pursuit of resources had a profound impact on African nations.

From an economic perspective, resource extraction became the backbone of European colonial economies. African nations were reduced to mere suppliers of raw materials, which were shipped back to Europe to fuel industrialization. This one-sided economic relationship left African countries dependent on exports, hindering their own industrial development and perpetuating a cycle of underdevelopment.

The environmental consequences of this exploitation cannot be overlooked either. European colonizers plundered Africa's forests, depleting valuable timber resources and causing irreversible damage to fragile ecosystems. Mining activities also took a toll on the environment, with toxic chemicals polluting rivers and soil, leading to long-term ecological degradation.

The social and cultural consequences of resource exploitation were equally profound. Many indigenous communities were displaced from their ancestral lands to make way for mining and agricultural projects. This displacement disrupted traditional ways of life and led to the erosion of cultural practices and identities. Additionally, the influx of European settlers disrupted social structures and created tensions between ethnic groups, further exacerbating existing divisions.

The political effects of resource exploitation were also significant. European colonial powers often divided African territories without regard for pre-existing ethnic boundaries, leading to the partitioning of ethnic groups and subsequent conflicts. This artificial division created a legacy of ethnic tensions that still plague many African nations today.

Furthermore, the exploitation of resources often came at the expense of human rights. Indigenous populations were subjected to forced labor, displacement, and even violence, as European colonizers sought to maximize their profits. This disregard for human rights further exacerbated the inequalities and disparities already present in African societies.

In conclusion, the exploitation of natural resources by European colonizers had profound and lasting effects on Africa. The economic, social, political, and environmental consequences of this exploitation continue to shape the continent today. By understanding and acknowledging this history, we can better comprehend the challenges faced by African nations and work towards a more equitable and sustainable future.

Disruption of Traditional African Economies

The disruption of traditional African economies is a crucial aspect to consider when examining the effects of European colonialism on African national borders. Historians have identified the immense economic impacts that colonization had on African nations, ultimately altering traditional economic systems and leading to long-lasting consequences.

Prior to European colonization, African economies were diverse and varied across the continent. Traditional economic systems were often based on subsistence farming, herding, and trading within local communities. However, with the arrival of European powers, these traditional economies were severely disrupted.

One of the primary ways in which traditional African economies were disrupted was through the imposition of cash crop production. European colonizers introduced cash crops such as cocoa, coffee, and rubber, which were grown for export to Europe. As a result, local communities were forced to shift their focus from subsistence farming to cash crop production, leading to a loss of self-sufficiency and increased dependence on the global market.

Furthermore, the establishment of European-controlled mines and plantations further disrupted traditional African economies. Indigenous people were often forced into labor-intensive work in these industries, leading to the exploitation of their resources and labor. This exploitation not only resulted in economic inequalities but also depleted natural resources and disrupted traditional agricultural practices.

The introduction of currencies by European colonizers also had a significant impact on traditional economies. African nations were required to adopt the currencies of their colonizers, which often led to inflation and economic instability. Additionally, the imposition of European trade practices and tariffs hindered local trade networks and limited the economic opportunities available to indigenous communities.

The disruption of traditional African economies had far-reaching social and cultural consequences. Indigenous communities that were once self-sufficient were forced into economic dependence and faced significant challenges in maintaining their cultural practices and traditions. Moreover, the economic disparities caused by colonization have persisted into the post-colonial era, leading to social inequalities and tensions within African nations.

In conclusion, the disruption of traditional African economies due to European colonialism has had profound and lasting effects. The shift from subsistence farming to cash crop production, the exploitation of resources, the introduction of foreign currencies, and the imposition of European trade practices have all contributed to economic disparities and cultural disruptions. Understanding these impacts is crucial for historians studying the effects of European colonialism on African national borders and the subsequent challenges faced by ethnic groups in post-colonial Africa.

Imposition of Trade and Economic Policies by European Powers

During the era of European colonialism in Africa, the imposition of trade and economic policies by European powers had a profound impact on the continent. This subchapter explores the consequences of these policies on various aspects of African societies, including the effects on national borders, ethnic groups, economies, cultures, politics, environment, human rights, education, healthcare, migration, and identity.

The European powers, such as Britain, France, Germany, and Portugal, sought to exploit Africa's vast resources and establish profitable trade routes. As a result, they imposed trade and economic policies that favored their own interests, often at the expense of African nations. These policies included the establishment of exclusive trade monopolies, high tariffs on African goods, forced labor, and the extraction of raw materials.

One of the major effects of these policies was the partitioning of African national borders, which was primarily driven by economic interests rather than considerations of ethnic and cultural affiliations. This led to the division of ethnic groups across different colonial territories, resulting in social and cultural consequences. Ethnic communities were separated, leading to the loss of traditional lands, disruption of cultural practices, and the creation of tension and conflict between different groups.

Moreover, the economic impacts of European colonialism on African nations were significant. The imposition of trade policies led to the underdevelopment of local industries and the dependence on exporting raw materials. This exploitative economic system hindered the growth of African economies, perpetuating poverty and inequality.

The political effects of European colonialism on ethnic groups in Africa were also far-reaching. The arbitrary drawing of national borders often disregarded the existing ethnic and tribal structures, leading to the marginalization and exclusion of certain groups. This fueled ethnic conflicts and tensions, which have persisted even after independence.

Additionally, the environmental consequences of European colonialism and the imposition of national borders in Africa were severe. The extraction of resources and deforestation for agricultural purposes resulted in ecological degradation, loss of biodiversity, and the destruction of natural habitats.

The partitioning of ethnic groups in Africa also had human rights implications. The forced displacement of communities, along with the denial of their rights to self-determination, resulted in the violation of human rights and the suppression of cultural identities.

Furthermore, European colonialism and the imposition of national borders had a detrimental impact on education and healthcare in African nations. Educational disparities and inequalities emerged, as colonial powers favored the education of certain groups over others. Similarly, healthcare challenges arose, as resources were unequally distributed, and certain ethnic groups faced limited access to healthcare services.

The imposition of trade and economic policies also led to migration patterns and the displacement of ethnic populations. Many communities were uprooted from their ancestral lands and forced to migrate to other regions, resulting in the loss of cultural heritage and the breakdown of social structures.

Lastly, the struggles for identity and self-determination among ethnic groups affected by European colonialism in Africa persist to this day. The legacy of colonialism continues to shape contemporary debates on national borders, citizenship rights, and the recognition of ethnic identities.

In conclusion, the imposition of trade and economic policies by European powers during colonialism had far-reaching effects on Africa. From the partitioning of national borders to the displacement of ethnic populations, the consequences of these policies continue to shape the social, economic, political, cultural, environmental, and human rights landscape of post-colonial Africa. Understanding these impacts is crucial for historians studying the effects of European colonialism on African national borders and its lasting implications for the continent.

Chapter 3: Social and Cultural Consequences of National Borders in Post-Colonial Africa

Fragmentation of Ethnic Groups and Communities

The fragmentation of ethnic groups and communities is a significant consequence of European colonialism on African national borders. This subchapter explores the various implications of this fragmentation, including its economic, social, cultural, political, environmental, human rights, educational, healthcare, migration, and identity-related effects.

Under the colonial rule, European powers drew arbitrary borders across Africa, often disregarding the traditional territories and ethnic boundaries of the indigenous populations. As a result, numerous ethnic groups found themselves divided between different nations, or worse, split into multiple countries. This haphazard partitioning created a multitude of challenges for these communities.

Economically, the division of ethnic groups disrupted traditional trade networks and economic systems, leading to a loss of livelihoods and economic disparities. Additionally, the imposition of European economic systems and exploitative policies further marginalized certain ethnic groups, exacerbating economic inequalities.

Socially and culturally, the national borders imposed by colonial powers disrupted long-standing kinship ties, cultural practices, and social cohesion. Communities that shared common histories, languages, and customs were fragmented, leading to a loss of cultural heritage and creating tensions among different ethnic groups.

Politically, the partitioning of ethnic groups resulted in the imposition of colonial governments and systems that favored certain ethnicities over others, leading to power struggles, ethnic conflicts, and political instability in post-colonial Africa.

Environmentally, the arbitrary borders often ignored ecological boundaries, leading to the division of natural ecosystems and resources, contributing to environmental degradation and resource disputes among neighboring countries.

The human rights issues resulting from the partitioning of ethnic groups in Africa cannot be overlooked. Minority ethnic groups often faced discrimination, marginalization, and exclusion from political power, leading to social injustices and human rights abuses.

Education and healthcare disparities emerged due to the division of ethnic groups. Access to quality education and healthcare services became unequal across different regions, perpetuating social and economic inequalities.

The partitioning of ethnic groups also resulted in forced migrations and displacement of populations, as people found themselves on the wrong side of the newly drawn borders. This created refugee crises, ethnic tensions, and conflicts that continue to impact the region to this day.

Furthermore, the struggle for identity and self-determination among ethnic groups affected by European colonialism in Africa remains a significant challenge. Individuals and communities have had to navigate multiple national identities, often leading to a loss of a sense of belonging and cultural identity.

In conclusion, the fragmentation of ethnic groups and communities caused by European colonialism in Africa has had far-reaching and multi-dimensional effects. Understanding these consequences is crucial for historians and those interested in the effects of European colonialism on African national borders, as well as the various niches associated with this topic.

Loss of Traditional Cultural Practices and Identity

The effects of European colonialism on African national borders have had profound consequences on the cultural practices and identity of the continent's diverse ethnic groups. This subchapter explores the various ways in which traditional cultural practices and identity have been eroded as a result of colonialism and the subsequent partitioning of ethnic groups in Africa.

One of the most significant impacts of European colonialism on traditional cultural practices is the imposition of Western norms and values. As colonial powers sought to exert control over African territories, they often enforced their own cultural practices and ideologies, thereby diminishing the importance of indigenous traditions. This resulted in the erosion of traditional beliefs, rituals, and customs that had been passed down through generations.

Moreover, the partitioning of ethnic groups and the creation of arbitrary national borders have further undermined traditional cultural practices and identity. Many ethnic groups found themselves divided across multiple countries, often separated from their ancestral lands and cultural heritage. The imposition of new borders disrupted long-established social networks and led to the fragmentation of communities, making it difficult for individuals to maintain their cultural identities.

Furthermore, the economic impacts of European colonialism have also contributed to the loss of traditional cultural practices. The introduction of cash crops and the exploitation of Africa's natural resources disrupted traditional subsistence economies, forcing many communities to abandon their traditional livelihoods and adopt Western economic practices. This transition often led to the abandonment of traditional cultural practices that were closely tied to subsistence farming and traditional economic systems.

The social and cultural consequences of national borders in post-colonial Africa have also played a significant role in eroding traditional cultural practices. The creation of new nation-states with distinct borders often resulted in the marginalization of ethnic minority groups. These groups, faced with discrimination and limited access to resources, were often forced to assimilate into the dominant culture, abandoning their own cultural practices in the process.

In conclusion, the loss of traditional cultural practices and identity in Africa can be attributed to the effects of European colonialism and the subsequent partitioning of ethnic groups. The imposition of Western values, the creation of arbitrary national borders, and the economic, social, and cultural consequences of colonial rule have all contributed to the erosion of traditional cultural practices and the fragmentation of ethnic identities. Understanding these processes is crucial for historians studying the effects of European colonialism on African national borders and the long-lasting impacts on the continent's diverse ethnic groups.

Challenges of Nation-Building and Development

Introduction:

The process of nation-building and development in Africa has been deeply influenced by the effects of European colonialism on national borders. This subchapter delves into the multifaceted challenges faced by African nations in their journey towards progress. From economic impacts to social and cultural consequences, political effects to environmental consequences, this section explores the wide-ranging issues that have shaped the post-colonial African landscape.

Economic Impacts of European Colonialism:

European colonialism in Africa had far-reaching economic consequences, with long-lasting effects on African nations. The exploitative practices of colonial powers disrupted traditional African economies, leading to resource extraction, forced labor, and the destruction of local industries. These economic disruptions continue to hamper development efforts in many African countries.

Social and Cultural Consequences of National Borders:

The partition of ethnic groups through the imposition of European colonial borders has had profound social and cultural consequences. Communities that were once united found themselves divided, leading to the fragmentation of cultural identities and eroding social cohesion. This subchapter explores the challenges faced by African nations in fostering unity and reconciliation among ethnically diverse populations.

Political Effects of European Colonialism:

The legacy of European colonialism on political systems in Africa is undeniable. The arbitrary drawing of national borders disregarded existing ethnic boundaries, resulting in the formation of multi-ethnic states with deep-rooted political tensions. This section analyzes the complexities of governing diverse populations and the challenges faced by African nations in establishing stable political structures.

Environmental Consequences of European Colonialism:

European colonialism in Africa also had severe environmental consequences. The exploitation of natural resources, deforestation, and unsustainable agricultural practices disrupted ecosystems and led to long-term environmental degradation. This subchapter explores the environmental challenges faced by African nations and the efforts being made to promote sustainable development and conservation.

Human Rights Issues Resulting from the Partitioning of Ethnic Groups:

The partitioning of ethnic groups during colonial times gave rise to numerous human rights issues. This section examines the struggles faced by ethnic minorities in terms of discrimination, marginalization, and the denial of basic human rights. It also highlights the importance of addressing these issues to achieve social justice and inclusivity.

Conclusion:

The challenges of nation-building and development in Africa are deeply intertwined with the effects of European colonialism on national borders. This subchapter sheds light on the economic, social, cultural, political, environmental, and human rights challenges faced by African nations. By understanding these challenges, historians and researchers can contribute to a more comprehensive understanding of Africa's post-colonial journey and the complexities of building prosperous and inclusive nations.

Chapter 4: Political Effects of European Colonialism on Ethnic Groups in Africa

Imposition of Colonial Administrations and Political Structures

The imposition of colonial administrations and political structures in Africa during the era of European colonialism had far-reaching and profound effects on the continent. This subchapter explores the various consequences of this imposition, focusing on the impact it had on national borders, ethnic groups, economies, societies, cultures, politics, environments, human rights, education, healthcare, migration patterns, and identities.

European colonial powers, driven by economic interests and a desire for territorial control, carved up Africa without regard for pre-existing ethnic boundaries. National borders were drawn haphazardly, leading to the partitioning of ethnic groups across multiple nations. This division had lasting consequences, as it disrupted traditional social structures and created tensions and conflicts between different ethnic communities.

The economic impacts of European colonialism on African nations were significant. Colonizers exploited Africa's resources, leading to the extraction of valuable minerals and agricultural products. This exploitation often led to environmental degradation and economic inequality, as the benefits of these resources were not evenly distributed among the local populations.

Social and cultural consequences were also evident in post-colonial Africa. The imposition of national borders disrupted traditional social networks and kinship ties, leading to the breakdown of communal bonds. Cultural practices and languages were suppressed, as European colonial powers enforced their own languages and cultural norms. This cultural suppression led to a loss of identity and self-determination struggles among affected ethnic groups.

The imposition of colonial administrations also had political effects on ethnic groups in Africa. European powers established centralized systems of governance, often favoring certain ethnic groups over others. This created power imbalances and fueled ethnic tensions and conflicts, which continue to be a challenge in post-colonial Africa.

The environmental consequences of European colonialism and national borders in Africa were significant. Resource exploitation and deforestation have led to ecological degradation and the loss of biodiversity. Traditional land-use practices were disrupted, leading to the displacement of indigenous populations and a loss of their connection to their ancestral lands.

Human rights issues resulting from the partitioning of ethnic groups in Africa are a grave concern. Many ethnic communities were forcibly displaced, resulting in the violation of their basic human rights. Discrimination, marginalization, and violence against these displaced populations are still prevalent in many African countries today.

Educational disparities and inequalities due to European colonialism and national borders in Africa are also evident. European colonial powers prioritized education for their own interests, neglecting the educational needs of local populations. This has resulted in significant disparities in educational attainment, with certain ethnic groups having limited access to quality education.

Health and healthcare challenges faced by ethnic groups in partitioned African countries are another consequence of colonial rule. Limited access to healthcare facilities, lack of resources, and inadequate healthcare infrastructure have all contributed to the poor health outcomes of many ethnic communities.

Migration patterns and displacement of ethnic populations as a result of colonial borders have been widespread. Many ethnic groups found themselves on the wrong side of national borders, leading to forced migration and displacement. This has resulted in the loss of livelihoods, social dislocation, and increased vulnerability for these populations.

In conclusion, the imposition of colonial administrations and political structures in Africa had far-reaching effects on national borders, ethnic groups, economies, societies, cultures, politics, environments, human rights, education, healthcare, migration patterns, and identities. Understanding these effects is crucial for historians studying the impact of European colonialism on the African continent.

Ethnic Divisions and Power Struggles in Post-Colonial Governments

In the aftermath of European colonialism in Africa, the continent was left with a complex tapestry of national borders that had significant implications for its ethnic groups. This subchapter explores the ethnic divisions and power struggles that emerged in post-colonial governments, shedding light on the lasting effects of European colonialism on African national borders.

One of the most profound impacts of colonialism was the partitioning of ethnic groups across different nations. European powers often drew national borders without considering the intricacies of ethnic identities and territories. As a result, many ethnic groups found themselves divided among multiple countries, while others were grouped together in a single nation. These artificial boundaries ignited long-standing tensions and conflicts, as ethnic communities struggled to assert their rights and maintain their cultural identities.

The political effects of European colonialism on ethnic groups in Africa were far-reaching. Post-colonial governments often favored one ethnic group over others, leading to power struggles and the marginalization of certain communities. This manipulation of power dynamics fueled ethnic tensions and hindered national unity, impeding the development and stability of these newly independent nations.

Moreover, the social and cultural consequences of national borders in post-colonial Africa were significant. The partitioning of ethnic groups disrupted traditional social structures and customs, leaving communities fractured and struggling to preserve their cultural heritage. Educational disparities and inequalities emerged as some ethnic groups received more resources and opportunities than others, perpetuating social and economic imbalances.

The environmental consequences of European colonialism and national borders in Africa were also profound. Natural resources were often divided along colonial borders, leading to disputes and conflicts over land and wealth. Additionally, the partitioning of ethnic groups disrupted longstanding patterns of migration and land use, resulting in environmental degradation and loss of biodiversity.

The partitioning of ethnic groups in Africa also gave rise to human rights issues. Forced displacement and migration patterns caused by colonial borders resulted in the displacement of ethnic populations, leading to the loss of homes, land, and livelihoods. Many ethnic groups faced discrimination and violence, while others struggled to assert their right to self-determination.

In conclusion, the effects of European colonialism on African national borders have had far-reaching consequences for ethnic groups in post-colonial governments. The legacy of ethnic divisions and power struggles continues to shape the political, social, and cultural landscape of these nations. Understanding and addressing these issues is crucial for historians and scholars interested in the impacts of European colonialism on African nations and the struggles faced by affected ethnic groups.

Challenges of Democracy and Governance

Introduction:

In the wake of European colonialism in Africa, the continent experienced a profound transformation that left a lasting impact on its political, social, economic, and cultural landscapes. This subchapter, titled "Challenges of Democracy and Governance," delves into the intricate web of issues that arose as a result of European colonialism and the partitioning of national borders in Africa. Addressing a diverse audience of historians and focusing on the effects of colonialism on African national borders, this subchapter aims to shed light on the numerous challenges faced by African nations in their pursuit of democracy and effective governance.

Political Effects of European Colonialism on Ethnic Groups in Africa:

One of the significant challenges emerging from European colonialism was the arbitrary drawing of national borders, disregarding the complex ethnic, cultural, and linguistic identities of African communities. This resulted in the partitioning of ethnic groups across multiple countries, leading to political instability, identity struggles, and ethnic conflict. Historians will explore the consequences of such divisions, analyzing the impact on self-determination struggles, political representation, and the formation of inclusive democratic institutions.

Social and Cultural Consequences of National Borders in Post-Colonial Africa:

The partitioning of African nations also had far-reaching social and cultural implications. Historians will delve into the complexities of identity formation and the erosion of traditional cultural practices as a consequence of colonial borders. They will examine how ethnic tensions caused by national borders have affected social cohesion, intergroup relations, and the preservation of cultural heritage.

Economic Impacts of European Colonialism on African Nations:

European colonial powers exploited African resources, leaving a legacy of economic dependency and underdevelopment. Historians will analyze how this has hindered the economic progress of African nations, contributing to disparities, inequalities, and limited access to resources. They will explore the challenges faced in establishing and maintaining sustainable economic systems, as well as the impact on healthcare, education, and migration patterns.

Health and Healthcare Challenges Faced by Ethnic Groups in Partitioned African Countries:

The partitioning of ethnic groups has had significant implications for healthcare systems. Historians will examine the challenges faced by ethnic populations in accessing healthcare services, including inadequate infrastructure, limited resources, and disparities in healthcare provision. The subchapter will shed light on the consequences of these challenges on the health and well-being of affected communities.

Conclusion:

This subchapter has highlighted the multifaceted challenges that emerged from European colonialism and the subsequent partitioning of national borders in Africa. Historians engaged in the study of the effects of colonialism on African national borders will gain a deeper understanding of the challenges faced by African nations in their pursuit of democracy and good governance. By examining the political, social, economic, and cultural dimensions, this subchapter aims to contribute to a comprehensive analysis of the complex tapestry woven by European colonialism and its enduring effects on African nations.

Chapter 5: Environmental Consequences of European Colonialism and National Borders in Africa

Destruction and Degradation of Natural Resources

The subchapter "Destruction and Degradation of Natural Resources" explores the devastating impact of European colonialism on the natural resources of African nations. This chapter delves into the historical context, examining the consequences of European colonization on the environment and its lasting effects on post-colonial Africa.

European colonial powers, driven by their economic interests, exploited Africa's rich natural resources, leading to widespread destruction and degradation. The extraction of minerals, such as gold, diamonds, and rubber, resulted in massive deforestation, land degradation, and pollution. Forests were cleared to make way for plantations, disrupting delicate ecosystems and eradicating biodiversity.

The economic impacts of this resource exploitation were twofold. On one hand, European powers profited immensely, fueling their industrialization and economic growth. On the other hand, African nations were left impoverished, unable to benefit from their own resources. This economic disparity continues to plague many African countries to this day.

The environmental consequences of European colonialism and the subsequent partitioning of national borders in Africa have been profound. The loss of forests and degradation of land has disrupted natural water cycles, leading to droughts, soil erosion, and desertification. These environmental challenges have affected agricultural productivity, food security, and the livelihoods of local communities.

Moreover, the destruction of natural habitats has threatened the survival of numerous plant and animal species, some of which are endemic to Africa. This loss of biodiversity not only diminishes the continent's ecological integrity but also hampers its potential for sustainable development.

Furthermore, the degradation of natural resources has had detrimental effects on the health and well-being of ethnic groups in partitioned African countries. Contaminated water sources, air pollution, and exposure to hazardous substances have contributed to the spread of diseases and increased mortality rates, particularly among vulnerable populations.

Understanding the environmental consequences of European colonialism in Africa is crucial for historians, as it sheds light on the complex interplay between colonization, resource exploitation, and environmental degradation. By examining this chapter, historians can gain deeper insights into the long-lasting impact of European colonialism on the continent's natural resources and environmental challenges faced by African nations today.

Displacement of Indigenous Communities and Wildlife

Throughout the history of European colonialism in Africa, one of the most devastating consequences has been the displacement of indigenous communities and the disruption of wildlife habitats. This subchapter aims to shed light on the profound impact that the establishment of national borders has had on both human and non-human populations, and the subsequent challenges they have faced.

As European powers carved up the African continent during the late 19th and early 20th centuries, they paid little heed to the existing ethnic and cultural boundaries that had long shaped the lives of indigenous communities. The arbitrary drawing of national borders disregarded the complex web of relationships between different ethnic groups, resulting in the forced separation of communities that had shared territories and resources for centuries.

This displacement had profound social, economic, and political consequences. Indigenous communities suddenly found themselves living in unfamiliar territories, often without access to their traditional lands and resources. This led to a loss of cultural identity, as well as economic hardships as they struggled to adapt to new environments and find means of sustenance.

Furthermore, the establishment of national borders disrupted wildlife habitats and migration routes. Animals that once roamed freely across vast landscapes found their movements restricted, often leading to population declines and increased conflicts with humans over limited resources. This disruption of ecosystems had far-reaching consequences for biodiversity and the delicate balance of African ecosystems.

The displacement of indigenous communities and wildlife also had severe human rights implications. Forced relocation often resulted in the violation of basic rights, including the right to self-determination and the right to a dignified life. Indigenous peoples were often subjected to discrimination, marginalization, and exploitation in their new environments, exacerbating existing inequalities.

Additionally, the displacement of indigenous communities contributed to ethnic tensions and conflicts in post-colonial Africa. Displaced populations often found themselves in close proximity to other ethnic groups, leading to competition over resources and increased cultural clashes.

In conclusion, the displacement of indigenous communities and wildlife as a result of European colonialism and the establishment of national borders in Africa has had far-reaching consequences. From social and economic hardships to environmental degradation and human rights violations, the effects of this displacement continue to shape the lives of African communities today. It is crucial for historians and those interested in African colonial history to understand and acknowledge these issues in order to work towards a more equitable and sustainable future.

Climate Change and Environmental Inequities

Introduction:

The effects of European colonialism on African national borders have had far-reaching consequences across various domains. One such domain that has been severely impacted is the environment. This subchapter will delve into the intertwining relationship between climate change and environmental inequities in post-colonial Africa. By examining the historical context and its implications, we aim to shed light on the environmental challenges faced by different ethnic groups as a result of European colonialism.

Historical Context:

European colonial powers, in their pursuit of economic gains, often exploited Africa's natural resources without considering the long-term consequences. The extraction of timber, minerals, and other valuable resources contributed to deforestation, land degradation, and pollution. These practices disrupted the delicate ecological balance and led to the loss of biodiversity.

Climate Change:

The environmental degradation caused by colonialism has exacerbated the impact of climate change on African nations. Rising temperatures, changing rainfall patterns, and increased frequency of extreme weather events like droughts and floods have had devastating effects on both the environment and human populations. Ethnic groups residing in vulnerable regions often bear the brunt of these climate-related disasters, further exacerbating existing inequalities.

Environmental Inequities:

The partitioning of ethnic groups through colonial borders has resulted in unequal access to natural resources, exacerbating environmental inequities. In many cases, minority ethnic groups have been marginalized and forced into environmentally vulnerable areas with limited access to resources. This has led to conflicts over land and water, as well as disparities in environmental management and conservation efforts.

Health and Livelihood Challenges:

The environmental consequences of colonialism have also had significant health and livelihood implications. Ethnic groups living in environmentally degraded regions often face challenges such as food insecurity, water scarcity, and exposure to pollution, which increase the risk of diseases and affect overall well-being. Additionally, the loss of traditional livelihoods and cultural practices further compounds these challenges.

Conclusion:

The intertwining relationship between climate change and environmental inequities in post-colonial Africa cannot be ignored. The effects of European colonialism on African national borders have had lasting consequences on the environment, exacerbating existing inequalities among ethnic groups. Recognizing and addressing these issues is crucial for achieving environmental justice and sustainable development in the continent. By understanding the historical context and its implications, historians can contribute to a comprehensive understanding of the multifaceted impacts of European colonialism on Africa's environment.

Chapter 6: Human Rights Issues Resulting from the Partitioning of Ethnic Groups in Africa

Forced Assimilation and Cultural Suppression

European colonialism in Africa had profound effects on the national borders of African countries. One of the most impactful consequences was forced assimilation and cultural suppression. This subchapter explores the devastating consequences of these practices, shedding light on the long-lasting effects they have had on the continent.

The European colonizers believed in the superiority of their own cultures and saw it as their mission to civilize the African populations. As a result, they imposed their language, religion, and customs on the indigenous people, often through violent means. This forced assimilation led to the erasure of indigenous languages, traditions, and ways of life, leaving a lasting impact on the cultural fabric of African societies.

Cultural suppression not only denied African communities the right to preserve their heritage, but it also fractured their sense of identity. The imposition of European values and norms created a divide between generations, with younger Africans growing up detached from their own cultural roots. This loss of identity has had far-reaching consequences, contributing to a sense of alienation and a struggle for self-determination among affected ethnic groups.

Furthermore, forced assimilation and cultural suppression have perpetuated educational disparities and inequalities in post-colonial Africa. European colonizers prioritized their own education systems, often neglecting the development of indigenous educational institutions. As a result, generations of Africans were denied access to quality education, further exacerbating social and economic inequalities.

The health and well-being of ethnic groups in partitioned African countries have also been severely impacted. European colonialism disrupted traditional healthcare systems and introduced foreign diseases to the continent. Access to healthcare became unequal, with marginalized communities often lacking the necessary resources and infrastructure. This has led to ongoing healthcare challenges, including high rates of preventable diseases and limited access to medical services.

Forced assimilation and cultural suppression have also contributed to ethnic conflicts and tensions in post-colonial Africa. The arbitrary drawing of national borders by European colonizers often disregarded the complex ethnic and tribal dynamics of the continent. This has resulted in the displacement of ethnic populations, as well as a deep-rooted sense of injustice and resentment among affected communities.

In conclusion, forced assimilation and cultural suppression have had far-reaching and detrimental effects on African nations. The erasure of indigenous languages, traditions, and ways of life has had a lasting impact on the cultural and social fabric of the continent. The consequences of these practices, including educational disparities, healthcare challenges, and ethnic conflicts, continue to shape the lives of millions of Africans today. By understanding and acknowledging these historical injustices, we can work towards a more inclusive and equitable future for all.

Violations of Indigenous Rights and Land Dispossession

Introduction:

In the legacy of European colonialism in Africa, one cannot overlook the grave violations of indigenous rights and the widespread dispossession of land that occurred. This subchapter aims to delve into the multifaceted consequences of these violations, shedding light on the historical context, their impact on indigenous populations, and the long-lasting effects on African nations. As historians, it is crucial to understand the intricate interplay between European colonialism, land dispossession, and the resulting socio-political and economic ramifications.

Historical Context:

European colonization often entailed the imposition of arbitrary national borders, disregarding the complex ethno-cultural fabric of African societies. Indigenous communities, deeply rooted in their ancestral lands, faced profound challenges as their territories were forcibly taken away. This process was often accompanied by violence, coercion, and the displacement of whole communities.

Impact on Indigenous Peoples:

The violations of indigenous rights and land dispossession had devastating effects on the affected communities. Indigenous groups lost their autonomy, cultural heritage, and traditional ways of life. Forced evictions and land seizures disrupted agriculture, leading to food insecurity and economic instability. Moreover, the loss of land as a source of identity further marginalized these communities, perpetuating a cycle of inequality and discrimination.

Political and Social Consequences:

The imposition of national borders based on colonial interests intensified ethnic tensions and conflicts. Indigenous groups found themselves divided, often becoming minority populations within newly created nation-states. This fragmentation sowed the seeds of discord, as ethnic groups vied for political power, resources, and recognition. The resulting instability hindered social development, impeded nation-building efforts, and created lasting divisions within African societies.

Human Rights Issues and Displacement:

The partitioning of ethnic groups disrupted social cohesion and led to the violation of human rights. Forced displacement and migration patterns emerged as indigenous populations sought refuge from violence and persecution. The struggles for self-determination and identity among these groups persist to this day, as they grapple with the loss of their ancestral lands and cultures.

Conclusion:

The violations of indigenous rights and land dispossession during European colonialism in Africa have left an indelible mark on the continent's history. Understanding the numerous consequences of these violations is crucial for comprehending the complexities of post-colonial Africa. By acknowledging this dark chapter, historians can contribute to a more comprehensive understanding of the effects of European colonialism on African national borders, ethnic groups, economics, politics, culture, environment, and human rights. Only by unraveling this tapestry can we hope to address the challenges faced by indigenous communities and work towards a more inclusive and equitable future.

Challenges of Reconciliation and Restorative Justice

In the aftermath of European colonialism in Africa, one of the most pressing challenges faced by the continent is that of reconciliation and restorative justice. The effects of colonialism, particularly the partitioning of ethnic groups and the establishment of national borders, have had far-reaching consequences for African nations, impacting various aspects of society, culture, politics, economy, and the environment. Addressing these challenges requires a comprehensive understanding of the historical context and a commitment to healing the wounds inflicted by colonial rule.

One of the primary challenges is reconciling the deep-rooted ethnic conflicts and tensions caused by the arbitrary drawing of national borders by European colonizers. These borders often divided ethnic groups, forcing them into different nations and leading to a sense of displacement and marginalization. This has resulted in ongoing conflicts, as ethnic groups struggle to assert their identity and demand self-determination. Restorative justice mechanisms must be implemented to address these grievances and foster reconciliation among different ethnic communities.

Another significant challenge lies in the social and cultural consequences of national borders in post-colonial Africa. The partitioning of ethnic groups has disrupted traditional social structures and cultural practices, leading to the erosion of cultural identities and a loss of communal cohesion. Reconciliation efforts must therefore aim to restore cultural heritage, promote cultural diversity, and encourage dialogue among different ethnic communities.

Additionally, economic impacts resulting from European colonialism have created disparities and inequalities among African nations. The exploitative economic practices of colonial powers have left many African countries economically disadvantaged, with limited access to resources and opportunities. Reconciliation processes must address these economic inequalities and promote inclusive economic development to ensure a more equitable society.

Furthermore, the partitioning of ethnic groups has had detrimental environmental consequences. European colonial powers often exploited African resources without regard for the sustainability of the environment, leading to deforestation, soil degradation, and pollution. Reconciliation efforts must incorporate environmental restoration and sustainable development to safeguard the natural heritage of African nations.

In conclusion, the challenges of reconciliation and restorative justice in post-colonial Africa are multifaceted and interconnected. Addressing the effects of European colonialism on African national borders requires a holistic approach that considers the economic, social, cultural, political, environmental, and human rights dimensions. Historians must actively engage in understanding these challenges and contribute to the discourse surrounding reconciliation and restorative justice in order to foster healing, unity, and progress in Africa.

Chapter 7: Ethnic Conflict and Tensions Caused by National Borders in Post-Colonial Africa

Border Disputes and Secession Movements

The effects of European colonialism on African national borders are far-reaching and complex. One significant consequence of this colonial legacy is the prevalence of border disputes and secession movements across the continent. Historians studying the impact of European colonialism on Africa must delve into these issues to gain a comprehensive understanding of the continent's post-colonial history.

The partitioning of ethnic groups by European colonial powers has had profound implications for African nations. The arbitrary drawing of borders disregarded existing ethnic and cultural boundaries, leading to tensions and conflicts that persist to this day. Disputes over territorial claims and resource allocation continue to fuel secession movements, as marginalized groups seek self-determination and autonomy.

Economically, the imposition of colonial borders disrupted traditional trade routes and hindered economic integration. African nations were left with fragmented economies, reliant on exporting raw materials to their former colonial powers. This legacy of economic dependency continues to hinder development and exacerbate inequalities within and between nations.

The social and cultural consequences of national borders in post-colonial Africa are significant. Communities that were once closely interconnected now find themselves divided by artificial boundaries, leading to a loss of social cohesion and cultural exchange. The partitioning of ethnic groups has disrupted traditional ways of life and eroded cultural identities.

Politically, the legacy of European colonialism continues to shape power dynamics and governance structures in Africa. Ethnic divisions and rivalries, exacerbated by the imposition of colonial borders, have fueled conflict and political instability. These divisions have often been exploited by political elites, leading to authoritarianism, corruption, and a lack of democratic governance.

Furthermore, the environmental consequences of European colonialism and national borders in Africa cannot be ignored. The arbitrary drawing of borders disregarded ecological zones and disrupted natural resource management. This has led to environmental degradation, loss of biodiversity, and conflicts over access to resources such as water and land.

The partitioning of ethnic groups has also had severe human rights implications. Displacement, forced migration, and the creation of stateless populations have resulted in human rights abuses and marginalization. Ethnic tensions and conflicts have led to violence, discrimination, and violations of basic human rights.

Education and healthcare disparities are another consequence of European colonialism and national borders in Africa. Ethnic groups in partitioned countries often face unequal access to quality education and healthcare services. This perpetuates inequalities and hampers social development and economic progress.

Migration patterns and displacement of ethnic populations have been a direct result of colonial borders. People have been uprooted from their ancestral lands and forced to migrate in search of safety and economic opportunities. This has led to the formation of diaspora communities and has contributed to the complexity of border disputes and secession movements.

Finally, the struggles for identity and self-determination among ethnic groups affected by European colonialism in Africa remain ongoing.

Many communities continue to resist the imposition of colonial borders and assert their right to determine their own destiny. These struggles for self-determination are deeply rooted in the historical injustices of European colonialism and have important implications for the future of the continent.

In conclusion, the subchapter on Border Disputes and Secession Movements in "Unraveling the Tapestry: The Effects of European Colonialism on African National Borders" examines the multifaceted consequences of European colonialism on African nations. Addressing the niches of historians interested in the effects of European colonialism on African national borders and the partition of ethnic groups, this subchapter explores the economic, social, cultural, political, environmental, human rights, educational, healthcare, migration, and identity struggles resulting from the arbitrary drawing of colonial borders. By understanding the complexities of these issues, historians can gain valuable insights into the challenges and opportunities that continue to shape post-colonial Africa.

Ethnic Discrimination and Marginalization

Introduction:

The subchapter "Ethnic Discrimination and Marginalization" explores the profound impact of European colonialism on African national borders, specifically focusing on the partitioning of ethnic groups and the consequences that followed. This subchapter delves into the historical, social, economic, political, and cultural implications of ethnic discrimination and marginalization in post-colonial Africa. By examining these issues, historians can gain a comprehensive understanding of the multifaceted challenges faced by ethnic groups in the continent.

Historical Context:

European colonial powers, driven by their quest for power and resources, imposed artificial national borders on Africa during the infamous Scramble for Africa in the late 19th and early 20th centuries. These arbitrary divisions often disregarded existing ethnic, linguistic, and cultural boundaries, leading to the fragmentation of communities and the subsequent marginalization of certain groups.

Social and Cultural Consequences:

The partitioning of ethnic groups resulted in the disruption of social structures and cultural practices that had been established for centuries. Communities were forced to coexist with other ethnicities, leading to intergroup tensions, conflicts, and a loss of traditional identities. This subchapter explores the long-lasting effects of these social and cultural upheavals on the descendants of these ethnic groups.

Political Effects:

The imposition of European colonial borders also had profound political consequences. Ethnic groups were divided between multiple nations, often finding themselves as minorities within the newly created states. This subchapter examines the challenges faced by these marginalized groups in asserting their political rights, achieving self-determination, and participating in the governance of their respective nations.

Economic Impacts:

European colonialism significantly disrupted the economic systems of African countries, resulting in uneven development and economic disparities among different ethnic groups. This subchapter discusses the economic consequences of ethnic discrimination and marginalization, exploring the unequal distribution of resources, land ownership, and economic opportunities.

Environmental Consequences:

The arbitrary drawing of national borders during colonialism disregarded the ecological dynamics and natural resource distribution in Africa. This subchapter explores the environmental consequences of European colonialism, including the exploitation of natural resources, deforestation, and land degradation, which have disproportionately affected certain ethnic groups.

Conclusion:

By examining ethnic discrimination and marginalization resulting from European colonialism, historians gain a deeper understanding of the complex and interrelated challenges faced by African countries. This subchapter sheds light on the social, economic, political, and cultural consequences of national borders, emphasizing the need for comprehensive approaches to address the historical injustices and promote social cohesion within African nations. Understanding this history is crucial for addressing the present-day issues faced by ethnic groups in post-colonial Africa, and for fostering inclusive societies that uphold human rights, equality, and self-determination.

Peacebuilding and Conflict Resolution Efforts

In the wake of European colonialism in Africa, the continent was left with a legacy of national borders that often cut across ethnic groups and disrupted long-established social, cultural, and political structures. These boundaries, imposed by colonial powers, have had profound effects on African nations and their people. This subchapter explores the peacebuilding and conflict resolution efforts that have emerged in response to these challenges.

One of the key issues resulting from the partitioning of ethnic groups in Africa is the ethnic conflict and tensions that have arisen as a consequence. The imposition of artificial borders has led to the displacement of populations, fragmentation of communities, and competition for resources, all of which have fueled interethnic strife. In response, various local and international organizations have undertaken peacebuilding initiatives to foster dialogue, reconciliation, and cooperation among warring factions. These efforts aim to address the root causes of conflict and promote sustainable peace.

Moreover, the human rights issues stemming from the partitioning of ethnic groups in Africa have drawn attention from the international community. The arbitrary nature of colonial borders has often resulted in the marginalization and oppression of certain ethnic communities. Human rights organizations have worked tirelessly to raise awareness about these injustices and advocate for the rights and self-determination of affected populations. They have also supported legal and institutional reforms to rectify historical injustices and ensure the protection of human rights for all.

Additionally, the social and cultural consequences of national borders in post-colonial Africa have been immense. Communities that were once connected by shared heritage and cultural practices now find themselves separated by colonial boundaries. This has led to a loss of cultural cohesion and identity, as well as the erosion of traditional social systems. Efforts to address these challenges include cultural exchange programs, the revitalization of indigenous knowledge systems, and the promotion of cultural heritage preservation.

Furthermore, economic impacts resulting from European colonialism on African nations have exacerbated tensions and conflicts. Colonial powers often exploited Africa's resources for their own benefit, leaving behind an economic legacy of inequality, dependence, and underdevelopment. To address these challenges, initiatives focusing on economic empowerment, job creation, and sustainable development have been implemented. These efforts aim to promote economic inclusivity, reduce poverty, and foster shared prosperity.

In conclusion, the effects of European colonialism on African national borders have had far-reaching consequences. However, various peacebuilding and conflict resolution efforts have emerged to address the challenges created by the arbitrary partitioning of ethnic groups. Through these initiatives, historians and other stakeholders are working towards healing wounds, promoting dialogue, and creating a more peaceful and inclusive future for Africa.

Chapter 8: Educational Disparities and Inequalities Due to European Colonialism and National Borders in Africa

Inequitable Access to Education and Resources

Chapter 5: Inequitable Access to Education and Resources

Introduction:

The effects of European colonialism on African national borders have had far-reaching consequences that continue to shape the continent's present-day realities. One of the most significant areas affected by this colonial legacy is the inequitable access to education and resources. This subchapter will explore the historical context, consequences, and ongoing challenges related to this issue, shedding light on the complex interplay between colonial influences and the post-colonial realities faced by African nations.

Historical Context:

European colonial powers, driven by their self-interests, exploited Africa's vast resources, often leaving local populations marginalized and impoverished. The establishment of national borders, largely arbitrary and disregarding ethnic and cultural boundaries, further exacerbated these inequalities. Consequently, access to education and resources became heavily skewed, perpetuating a cycle of poverty and limited opportunities for certain ethnic groups.

Consequences:

The repercussions of inequitable access to education and resources are multi-faceted. Firstly, educational disparities persist, with marginalized ethnic groups facing limited access to quality education, resulting in lower literacy rates and diminished socio-economic prospects. This disparity perpetuates a cycle of poverty, hindering their ability to fully participate in the development of their societies.

Furthermore, limited access to resources, such as land, water, and healthcare, disproportionately affects marginalized ethnic groups. This leads to health disparities, as these communities face challenges in accessing essential healthcare services and suffer from higher rates of infectious diseases and malnutrition. The lack of access to resources also hinders economic development and perpetuates socio-economic inequalities.

Ongoing Challenges:

Addressing the inequitable access to education and resources requires a comprehensive approach. Governments and international organizations must prioritize investments in education, ensuring equal opportunities for all ethnic groups. This includes improving infrastructure, teacher training, and curriculum development to cater to diverse cultural needs.

Additionally, policies must be implemented to ensure equitable distribution of resources, particularly in areas with high concentrations of marginalized ethnic groups. This involves land reform, access to clean water, and improved healthcare infrastructure. By addressing these challenges, African nations can work towards creating inclusive societies that foster equal opportunities for all.

Conclusion:

The inequitable access to education and resources resulting from European colonialism and the establishment of national borders continues to be a pressing issue in post-colonial Africa. By understanding the historical context, consequences, and ongoing challenges, historians can contribute to the broader discourse on the effects of colonialism and advocate for policies that promote equitable access to education and resources. Only through collective efforts can Africa bridge these disparities and build a more inclusive and prosperous future for all its people.

Language Barrier and Cultural Bias in Education

Introduction:

In the aftermath of European colonialism in Africa, the effects of national borders have been far-reaching and extensive. This subchapter aims to shed light on the language barrier and cultural bias in education that emerged as a consequence of European colonial rule. By exploring this facet, historians can gain a deeper understanding of the educational disparities and inequalities that continue to plague post-colonial African nations.

Language Barrier:

European colonial powers imposed their languages on African territories, relegating indigenous languages to secondary status. This linguistic imposition created a significant language barrier in education. Local populations, who primarily spoke their native languages, were forced to learn and be educated in foreign languages such as English, French, or Portuguese. Consequently, this language barrier hindered effective communication, comprehension, and ultimately, the quality of education received by African students.

Cultural Bias:

European colonialism brought about cultural biases in education that perpetuated inequality. Education systems were designed to promote European cultural values, history, and literature while disregarding local traditions, knowledge systems, and indigenous languages. This cultural bias not only undermined the self-esteem and identity of African students but also perpetuated a Eurocentric worldview, which hindered the development of a genuinely inclusive and holistic education system.

Implications:

The language barrier and cultural bias in education have had profound implications for post-colonial Africa. Firstly, educational disparities and inequalities persist, with those who are proficient in European languages having a significant advantage over their peers. This perpetuates social and economic inequalities, limiting opportunities for upward mobility and hindering the overall development of African nations.

Furthermore, the neglect of indigenous languages and cultural knowledge systems has led to a loss of cultural heritage and identity among African populations. This, in turn, has contributed to a diminished sense of self-determination and weakened social cohesion within ethnic groups.

Conclusion:

The language barrier and cultural bias in education resulting from European colonialism have had long-lasting consequences on post-colonial African nations. Historians must recognize and address these issues to gain a comprehensive understanding of the effects of European colonialism on national borders in Africa. By acknowledging the educational disparities and inequalities caused by language barriers and cultural biases, efforts can be made to promote inclusive and equitable education systems that honor and incorporate the rich cultural diversity of Africa.

Empowering Education for Sustainable Development

Education plays a crucial role in addressing the multifaceted effects of European colonialism on African national borders. It is through education that historians can unravel the complex tapestry of colonialism's impact on ethnic groups, economies, societies, cultures, politics, environments, human rights, health, migration, and identity. This subchapter aims to highlight the importance of empowering education for sustainable development in post-colonial Africa.

The effects of European colonialism on African national borders were far-reaching and continue to shape the continent's trajectory. Historians have extensively researched the partitioning of ethnic groups, which led to the creation of artificial borders that disregarded traditional territories and cultural ties. These borders, imposed by colonizers without considering the ethnic, linguistic, and historical affinities of African communities, resulted in social, political, and economic divisions that persist today.

Empowering education can help address these divisions by fostering a sense of shared history and identity among diverse ethnic groups. By incorporating the study of pre-colonial African societies and the impact of European colonialism into the curriculum, historians can contribute to a more inclusive and accurate understanding of African history. This knowledge can empower individuals to challenge the divisive narratives perpetuated by colonial borders and work towards unity and cooperation.

Furthermore, education can be a powerful tool to address the economic disparities caused by colonialism. Historians can analyze the economic impact of European colonialism on African nations, including the extraction of resources and the imposition of exploitative economic systems. By teaching critical economic literacy skills, educators can equip individuals with the knowledge to challenge and overcome these legacies of colonialism, fostering sustainable economic development and reducing inequalities.

Education can also play a vital role in promoting social and cultural cohesion in post-colonial Africa. By incorporating diverse cultural perspectives into the curriculum, historians can foster respect and appreciation for the rich cultural heritage of various ethnic groups. This can contribute to the preservation of cultural traditions, languages, and customs that were marginalized during the colonial era.

Moreover, education can address the human rights issues resulting from the partitioning of ethnic groups in Africa. Historians can shed light on the violations committed against ethnic communities and advocate for justice and reparations. By teaching about human rights and promoting a culture of tolerance and inclusivity, education can empower individuals to challenge discriminatory practices and promote equality.

In conclusion, empowering education for sustainable development is vital to unraveling the effects of European colonialism on African national borders. By addressing the historical, economic, social, political, environmental, and cultural consequences of colonialism, education can foster unity, equality, and justice in post-colonial Africa. Historians have a crucial role to play in researching and disseminating knowledge that challenges the divisive legacies of colonialism, contributing to a more inclusive and equitable future for the continent.

Chapter 9: Health and Healthcare Challenges Faced by Ethnic Groups in Partitioned African Countries

Limited Access to Healthcare Services

The effects of European colonialism on African national borders have had far-reaching consequences across various aspects of society. One crucial area that has been profoundly impacted is access to healthcare services. The partitioning of ethnic groups and the establishment of national borders have resulted in numerous challenges and disparities in healthcare provision across the continent.

In post-colonial Africa, limited access to healthcare services has become a pressing issue. The creation of national borders often disregarded the existing social and cultural structures, dividing ethnic groups and disrupting traditional healthcare systems. As a result, many communities found themselves cut off from essential medical services, resulting in increased morbidity and mortality rates.

The economic impacts of European colonialism on African nations further exacerbated the healthcare challenges. Limited resources and underdeveloped healthcare infrastructure made it difficult to provide adequate medical care to all citizens. Additionally, the prioritization of economic interests by colonial powers often led to neglect of the healthcare sector, leaving it underfunded and ill-equipped to meet the growing needs of the population.

The political effects of European colonialism on ethnic groups in Africa also play a significant role in limiting access to healthcare services. In some cases, governments have prioritized certain regions or ethnic groups, leading to unequal distribution of healthcare resources. This has created disparities in healthcare access, with marginalized communities often being neglected.

The partitioning of ethnic groups and the resulting ethnic conflict and tensions have further hindered healthcare provision. Displacement of populations due to colonial borders has led to overcrowding in certain areas, straining already limited healthcare facilities. Moreover, ethnic conflicts have disrupted healthcare services, making it difficult for medical professionals to reach affected communities.

The environmental consequences of European colonialism and national borders in Africa have also impacted healthcare access. The division of land and resources has led to ecological degradation, resulting in the spread of diseases and the destruction of natural remedies used by traditional healers. This has further limited options for healthcare in affected communities.

Addressing the challenges of limited access to healthcare services requires a comprehensive approach. Governments and international organizations need to prioritize healthcare infrastructure development, ensuring adequate funding and resources are allocated to underserved areas. Additionally, efforts should be made to integrate traditional healing practices into the formal healthcare system, acknowledging their importance in certain communities.

In conclusion, limited access to healthcare services is a significant consequence of European colonialism and the partitioning of ethnic groups in Africa. The economic, social, political, and environmental impacts of colonialism have all contributed to the healthcare challenges faced by many communities. Addressing these disparities requires a multifaceted approach that takes into account the unique needs and cultural practices of different ethnic groups. Only through concerted efforts can we hope to overcome these challenges and ensure equitable access to healthcare for all.

Disease Outbreaks and Public Health Crises

Throughout history, disease outbreaks and public health crises have had a significant impact on African nations, particularly in the context of European colonialism and the partition of ethnic groups. This subchapter delves into the intricate relationship between disease outbreaks, public health crises, and the effects of European colonialism on African national borders.

European colonial powers, seeking to exploit Africa's resources and establish dominance, often disregarded existing ethnic boundaries when drawing national borders. This arbitrary division of ethnic groups disrupted social, cultural, and political structures, creating a fertile ground for disease outbreaks and public health crises. The imposition of colonial borders led to the fragmentation of ethnic communities, hindering their ability to respond effectively to health challenges.

One of the key consequences of colonial borders was the disruption of traditional healthcare systems. Indigenous healing practices and community-based healthcare networks were often disregarded or suppressed, leading to a loss of vital knowledge and resources. As a result, ethnic groups faced significant challenges in accessing quality healthcare, exacerbating the impact of disease outbreaks.

Moreover, the partitioning of ethnic groups created conditions for the spread of diseases. The arbitrary division of communities often separated families, disrupted trade routes, and hindered the free movement of people, goods, and information. This fragmentation impeded the implementation of coordinated public health strategies, making it difficult to contain and control the spread of diseases.

Disease outbreaks and public health crises also exacerbated existing social and economic inequalities resulting from European colonialism. Ethnic groups that were already marginalized and impoverished faced greater challenges in accessing healthcare, clean water, and sanitation facilities. Moreover, the economic exploitation by colonial powers often led to the depletion of natural resources, environmental degradation, and increased exposure to disease vectors.

This subchapter examines specific disease outbreaks and public health crises that occurred in the context of European colonialism and the partitioning of African ethnic groups. It analyzes the impact of these crises on healthcare systems, socioeconomic disparities, and the overall well-being of affected communities. By understanding the historical context and consequences of disease outbreaks, historians can gain insights into the complex interplay between European colonialism, national borders, and public health challenges in Africa.

Promoting Health Equity and Universal Healthcare

In the complex tapestry of European colonialism's effects on African national borders, one cannot overlook the profound impact on health and healthcare disparities among ethnic groups. The partitioning of African countries by colonial powers not only disrupted social and cultural structures but also had far-reaching consequences for the health and well-being of these communities.

One of the most pressing challenges resulting from colonial borders is the unequal access to healthcare. Ethnic groups that were divided by arbitrary lines experienced varying levels of healthcare infrastructure and services. This disparity has led to substantial health inequalities, with some communities having limited or no access to essential healthcare facilities, medications, and trained medical professionals.

Furthermore, the partitioning of ethnic groups has disrupted traditional healing practices and knowledge systems that were deeply rooted in cultural beliefs and practices. This loss of cultural heritage has had detrimental effects on the overall well-being and mental health of affected communities.

The environmental consequences of European colonialism, such as the exploitation of natural resources and deforestation, have also had severe health implications. Communities living in proximity to mining or extraction sites have been exposed to hazardous substances, leading to increased rates of respiratory diseases, cancers, and other health conditions.

The human rights issues resulting from the partitioning of ethnic groups in Africa are closely intertwined with the health challenges faced by these communities. Forced displacement and migration patterns have resulted in overcrowded refugee camps and inadequate healthcare provision, exacerbating the spread of infectious diseases and deteriorating the overall health of already vulnerable populations.

Addressing these health and healthcare challenges requires a commitment to promoting health equity and universal healthcare. Governments, non-governmental organizations, and international bodies must collaborate to ensure that all individuals, regardless of their ethnic background or geographical location, have access to quality healthcare services.

This can be achieved through the establishment of inclusive healthcare policies, the strengthening of healthcare infrastructure in underserved areas, and the training and deployment of healthcare professionals to remote and marginalized communities.

Moreover, efforts should be made to integrate traditional healing practices into the modern healthcare system, respecting the cultural beliefs and knowledge systems of affected communities. This holistic approach to healthcare can contribute to the overall well-being and resilience of these communities.

In conclusion, the effects of European colonialism on African national borders have had profound implications for the health and healthcare of ethnic groups. By promoting health equity and universal healthcare, we can begin to unravel the tapestry of colonialism's legacy and work towards a future where all individuals in Africa have equal access to quality healthcare services, regardless of their ethnic background or geographical location.

Chapter 10: Migration Patterns and Displacement of Ethnic Populations as a Result of Colonial Borders

Forced Migration and Refugee Crises

The subchapter "Forced Migration and Refugee Crises" delves into one of the most significant consequences of European colonialism on African national borders. This chapter explores the profound impact of colonial policies on ethnic groups, leading to forced migration and the emergence of refugee crises that persist to this day.

European colonial powers, driven by their quest for resources and geopolitical dominance, drew arbitrary borders across Africa during the infamous Scramble for Africa in the late 19th and early 20th centuries. These imposed borders disregarded the intricate social, cultural, and ethnic dynamics that had shaped African societies for centuries. Consequently, ethnic communities found themselves divided by these artificial boundaries, resulting in the displacement of millions.

The forced migration of ethnic populations had severe economic implications. Communities that were once self-sufficient were torn apart, disrupting traditional trade routes, agricultural practices, and economic systems. This upheaval led to economic instability and dependency on colonial powers, perpetuating a cycle of poverty that continues to afflict many African nations today.

Moreover, the partitioning of ethnic groups had significant social and cultural consequences. Communities that shared common languages, traditions, and customs were divided, eroding their cultural heritage and sense of identity. This fragmentation often resulted in intergroup tensions, ethnic conflicts, and the suppression of cultural practices by dominant groups.

The political effects of European colonialism on ethnic groups in Africa were also far-reaching. The imposition of colonial borders created artificial nation-states comprising multiple ethnicities, often leading to power struggles and political instability. These tensions, fueled by the legacy of colonialism, continue to plague many African nations, hindering their development and democratic progress.

Furthermore, the environmental consequences of colonialism and national borders in Africa cannot be overlooked. Dividing communities disrupted ecological balance, leading to unsustainable land use practices, deforestation, and resource exploitation. These environmental challenges exacerbate the vulnerability of ethnic populations, particularly those dependent on natural resources for their livelihoods.

The partitioning of ethnic groups in Africa also gave rise to human rights issues. Ethnic minorities often faced discrimination, marginalization, and exclusion from political and economic opportunities. This subchapter examines the struggles faced by these groups, shedding light on the need for human rights advocacy and social justice.

The forced migration and displacement of ethnic populations also had a profound impact on education and healthcare. The disruption caused by colonial borders resulted in educational disparities and inequalities, limiting access to quality education and healthcare services for many communities. This chapter explores the challenges faced by ethnic groups in these areas and highlights the need for targeted interventions to address these disparities.

Lastly, the subchapter explores the intricate patterns of migration and displacement that emerged as a result of colonial borders. Many ethnic groups were uprooted from their ancestral lands, leading to mass migrations and the creation of refugee crises. These migrations, both internal and across borders, continue to shape the demographic landscape of Africa and have significant implications for regional stability and security.

In conclusion, the subchapter "Forced Migration and Refugee Crises" highlights the devastating consequences of European colonialism on African national borders. It addresses the multifaceted effects on ethnic groups, including economic, social, cultural, political, environmental, and human rights dimensions. By examining these challenges, historians gain valuable insights into the complex legacy of colonialism and its implications for contemporary Africa.

Internal Displacement and Urbanization

One of the profound consequences of European colonialism in Africa is the issue of internal displacement and urbanization. This subchapter delves into the intricate relationship between these two phenomena, examining their historical roots, socio-economic implications, and human rights concerns.

The arbitrary drawing of national borders by European colonizers often resulted in the partitioning of ethnic groups, forcing people to leave their ancestral lands and seek refuge in unfamiliar territories. This displacement, in turn, led to the rapid growth of urban centers as people flocked to cities in search of safety and economic opportunities. The impact of internal displacement and urbanization on African societies cannot be overstated, as it fundamentally reshaped the social, cultural, economic, and political landscapes of post-colonial Africa.

From a socio-economic perspective, internal displacement and urbanization caused significant disruptions. Traditional livelihoods dependent on agriculture and pastoralism were abandoned, leading to the loss of cultural practices and knowledge. Additionally, the influx of displaced populations placed immense pressure on urban infrastructure, housing, and public services, exacerbating existing inequalities and creating new social challenges.

The human rights implications of internal displacement and urbanization are equally alarming. Displaced populations often faced discrimination, marginalization, and limited access to basic services such as healthcare and education. Their right to self-determination was compromised as they were forced to assimilate into unfamiliar urban environments.

Furthermore, the environmental consequences of internal displacement and urbanization cannot be ignored. The concentration of populations in urban areas resulted in increased pollution, depletion of natural resources, and the degradation of ecosystems. This, in turn, contributed to further inequalities and health disparities among affected ethnic groups.

Understanding the complex relationship between internal displacement and urbanization is crucial in unpacking the long-lasting effects of European colonialism on African national borders. By examining the historical, socio-economic, environmental, and human rights dimensions, historians can gain valuable insights into the multifaceted challenges faced by ethnic groups in post-colonial Africa. By shedding light on these issues, this subchapter aims to contribute to a comprehensive understanding of the impact of European colonialism on African nations and the partition of ethnic groups.

Addressing the Needs of Displaced Populations

In the complex tapestry of African history, the effects of European colonialism on national borders have had far-reaching consequences. One of the most pressing issues arising from this colonial legacy is the displacement of populations across the continent. This subchapter delves into the challenges faced by displaced populations and the need to address their needs.

The partitioning of ethnic groups resulting from European colonialism has had profound social, cultural, and political impacts in post-colonial Africa. Displaced populations often find themselves severed from their ancestral lands, uprooted from their communities, and forced to navigate unfamiliar territories. This disruption has led to a myriad of challenges, including ethnic conflict, tensions, and even human rights violations.

Furthermore, the economic consequences of colonialism have exacerbated the predicament of displaced populations. Limited access to resources and opportunities has hindered their economic well-being, perpetuating cycles of poverty and inequality. Educational disparities and healthcare challenges further compound their struggles, as they face obstacles in accessing quality education and healthcare services.

Migration patterns and displacement of ethnic populations have been a direct consequence of the arbitrary national borders drawn by European colonizers. This mass movement of people has created immense strain on host communities, often resulting in resource scarcity, strained infrastructure, and increased competition for limited resources. The environmental consequences of these population movements, such as deforestation and land degradation, further exacerbate the challenges faced by both displaced populations and host communities.

To address the needs of displaced populations, it is crucial to adopt a comprehensive and multi-faceted approach. Governments, international organizations, and civil society must work together to provide humanitarian assistance, develop sustainable livelihood programs, and promote social cohesion among affected communities. Efforts should focus on ensuring equitable access to education, healthcare, and economic opportunities for displaced populations.

Additionally, fostering dialogue and reconciliation among ethnic groups is vital to mitigate ethnic tensions and conflicts arising from the partitioning of African nations. Emphasizing the importance of respecting human rights and promoting inclusive governance structures can help address the underlying causes of displacement and facilitate the healing process.

In conclusion, the displacement of populations resulting from European colonialism in Africa is a complex issue that requires focused attention. By addressing the needs of displaced populations through comprehensive strategies, societies can strive towards reconciliation, social justice, and sustainable development. Only through these efforts can we begin to unravel the tapestry of colonialism's effects on African national borders and pave the way for a more inclusive and equitable future.

Chapter 11: Identity and Self-Determination Struggles Among Ethnic Groups Affected by European Colonialism in Africa

Reclaiming Cultural Identity and Heritage

In the wake of European colonialism and its lasting impact on African national borders, the struggle for ethnic groups to reclaim their cultural identity and heritage has become a pressing issue. Historians have delved into the multifaceted consequences of European colonization, shedding light on the social, cultural, political, economic, and environmental impacts that have shaped the continent.

One of the most significant effects of colonialism on African nations has been the partitioning of ethnic groups. This arbitrary division has disrupted traditional territories and led to the fragmentation of communities that shared common languages, customs, and histories. As a result, there has been a loss of cultural cohesion and a struggle to maintain cultural practices and traditions.

The economic impacts of European colonization have also been profound. The exploitation of African resources for the benefit of colonial powers has left many African nations economically disadvantaged. This has resulted in a loss of autonomy and the perpetuation of economic inequalities that continue to hinder development and prosperity.

Furthermore, the social and cultural consequences of national borders in post-colonial Africa cannot be ignored. The imposition of colonial borders has created artificial divisions among ethnic groups, leading to social tensions and conflicts. This has also contributed to the erosion of cultural identities, as ethnic groups face challenges in preserving their unique customs and traditions.

Politically, European colonialism has had a lasting impact on ethnic groups in Africa. The imposition of colonial rule and subsequent independence struggles have often led to power struggles and conflicts along ethnic lines. The partitioning of ethnic groups has fueled ethnic tensions and even violent conflicts in some cases.

The environmental consequences of European colonialism and the establishment of national borders in Africa have also been severe. The exploitation of natural resources without adequate regard for sustainability has led to environmental degradation and loss of biodiversity. This has further marginalized and displaced ethnic groups who rely on the land for their livelihoods and cultural practices.

The partitioning of ethnic groups in Africa has also resulted in numerous human rights issues. Ethnic minorities often face discrimination and exclusion, while forced displacement and migration patterns have uprooted communities and disrupted their way of life. This has led to struggles for identity and self-determination among affected ethnic groups.

Additionally, educational disparities, healthcare challenges, and migration patterns have further deepened the impact of European colonialism and national borders on ethnic groups. Educational opportunities have been unequal, healthcare access has been limited, and the forced migration of populations has led to social and economic dislocation.

In conclusion, the subchapter on "Reclaiming Cultural Identity and Heritage" explores the profound consequences of European colonialism and national borders on ethnic groups in Africa. It highlights the challenges faced by these groups in maintaining their cultural identity and heritage, and the various dimensions of the impact on their lives. This chapter aims to provide historians with a comprehensive understanding of the struggles faced by ethnic groups in post-colonial Africa and the importance of reclaiming cultural identity and heritage for future generations.

Independence Movements and Nation-States

Throughout the pages of history, the effects of European colonialism on African national borders have left an indelible mark on the continent. This subchapter, titled "Independence Movements and Nation-States," delves into the repercussions that have shaped the social, political, economic, and cultural landscapes of post-colonial Africa. Addressing a diverse audience of historians, this chapter aims to shed light on the multifaceted consequences of European colonialism in Africa and the subsequent partitioning of ethnic groups.

One of the most significant impacts of European colonialism was the creation of artificial national borders, disregarding pre-existing ethnic boundaries. This arbitrary division led to profound economic disparities within African nations. The exploitation of resources and the establishment of trade routes by European powers disrupted indigenous economies, leaving African nations grappling with a legacy of economic dependency and underdevelopment.

Moreover, the partitioning of ethnic groups had far-reaching social and cultural consequences. Communities that had shared histories, traditions, and languages found themselves divided by colonial borders, which often resulted in ethnic tensions and conflicts. This subchapter explores the human rights issues arising from the partitioning of ethnic groups, including forced displacement, loss of land and resources, and the erosion of cultural identity.

The political effects of colonialism on ethnic groups are examined, highlighting the challenges faced by post-colonial African nations in building inclusive and representative governments. Ethnic conflict and tensions, rooted in the hasty formation of nation-states, have hindered political stability and development.

The environmental consequences of colonialism are also explored. European powers exploited Africa's natural resources without consideration for the long-term impact on the environment, leading to deforestation, soil erosion, and the degradation of ecosystems. Understanding these environmental challenges is crucial for sustainable development and conservation efforts in present-day Africa.

Furthermore, this subchapter delves into the educational disparities and health challenges faced by ethnic groups in partitioned African countries. European colonialism disrupted traditional educational systems, resulting in unequal access to education, perpetuating social and economic inequalities. Additionally, partitioned nations struggle to provide adequate healthcare services to their populations, further exacerbating health disparities.

Migration patterns and displacement of ethnic populations as a consequence of colonial borders are discussed, highlighting the struggles faced by those uprooted from their ancestral lands. The subchapter also explores the identity and self-determination struggles among ethnic groups affected by European colonialism, emphasizing the importance of recognizing and respecting diverse cultural and ethnic identities.

In unraveling the tapestry of European colonialism on African national borders, this subchapter offers a comprehensive understanding of the complex effects that continue to shape the African continent. By delving into the economic, social, political, cultural, environmental, and human rights dimensions, historians can gain valuable insights into the lasting legacies of colonialism and its impact on ethnic groups in post-colonial Africa.

Decolonization and the Quest for Self-Determination

In the subchapter "Decolonization and the Quest for Self-Determination," we delve into the profound effects of European colonialism on African national borders and the subsequent struggle for self-determination. This chapter aims to provide historians with a comprehensive understanding of the multifaceted consequences of colonial rule, focusing on various niches such as the partition of ethnic groups, economic impacts, social and cultural consequences, political effects, environmental consequences, human rights issues, ethnic conflict and tensions, educational disparities and inequalities, health and healthcare challenges, migration patterns, and identity and self-determination struggles.

European colonialism in Africa had a profound impact on the national borders established on the continent. The partitioning of ethnic groups often disregarded their historical territories, leading to severe social, cultural, and political consequences. The imposed borders created divisions and conflicts among ethnic communities, as they were forced to coexist within newly drawn boundaries, often leading to ethnic tensions and conflicts that persist to this day.

The economic impacts of colonial rule were significant, as European powers exploited African resources for their own benefit. This exploitation resulted in vast disparities in wealth and development between colonizer and colonized. Post-colonial African nations faced numerous challenges in building sustainable economies, as they inherited an exploitative economic structure.

Moreover, the social and cultural consequences of national borders in post-colonial Africa cannot be understated. The artificial division of ethnic groups disrupted traditional social structures and cultural practices. It led to the erosion of cultural identities and a loss of cultural heritage, as communities were separated by arbitrary borders.

The political effects of European colonialism on ethnic groups in Africa were far-reaching. Colonial powers often favored certain ethnic groups, creating power imbalances that continue to shape political dynamics. This, coupled with the divisive national borders, has resulted in ongoing political instability and ethnic conflicts in many African nations.

The environmental consequences of colonialism and the establishment of national borders in Africa have been detrimental as well. The exploitation of natural resources by colonial powers often led to ecological degradation and the disruption of delicate ecosystems. Post-colonial governments have struggled to address these environmental challenges while balancing economic development.

The partitioning of ethnic groups and the imposition of national borders have also had severe human rights implications. Many ethnic groups found themselves divided between different nations, leading to displacement, loss of land, and the denial of basic human rights.

Educational disparities and inequalities resulting from colonialism and national borders have perpetuated social and economic inequalities. Ethnic communities have faced unequal access to education, resulting in a lack of opportunities and hindering their socio-economic development.

Health and healthcare challenges have also arisen due to the partitioning of ethnic groups. The division of communities has disrupted healthcare systems and led to unequal access to medical services, exacerbating health disparities among different ethnic groups.

The migration patterns and displacement of ethnic populations resulting from colonial borders have had a lasting impact on African societies. The forced movement of people and the creation of refugee populations have fueled ethnic tensions and conflicts, and have also strained resources and infrastructure in host nations.

Lastly, the struggle for self-determination and the quest for identity among ethnic groups affected by European colonialism in Africa have been ongoing. Many communities have fought for autonomy and recognition, seeking to assert their distinct culture, language, and traditions in the face of imposed borders.

In conclusion, the subchapter "Decolonization and the Quest for Self-Determination" provides historians with a comprehensive exploration of the effects of European colonialism on African national borders. By examining the partition of ethnic groups, economic impacts, social and cultural consequences, political effects, environmental consequences, human rights issues, ethnic conflict and tensions, educational disparities, health challenges, migration patterns, and struggles for self-determination, we gain a deeper understanding of the complex and lasting legacy of colonial rule on the African continent.

Conclusion: The Ongoing Legacy of European Colonialism on African National Borders.

Conclusion: The Ongoing Legacy of European Colonialism on African National Borders

The effects of European colonialism on African national borders have had a profound and lasting impact on the continent. As historians, it is crucial to understand and analyze the various facets of this legacy in order to gain a comprehensive understanding of Africa's past and present.

One of the key areas affected by colonialism was the partition of ethnic groups. European powers drew arbitrary borders without considering the ethnic, cultural, and linguistic diversity of the African people. This led to the fragmentation of ethnic groups across multiple countries, resulting in a loss of identity and self-determination struggles. The ongoing ethnic conflicts and tensions in post-colonial Africa can be traced back to these artificial borders.

Furthermore, the economic impacts of European colonialism on African nations cannot be ignored. The exploitation of resources, forced labor, and unequal trade policies have left many African countries in a state of economic dependency. The legacy of colonialism has hindered the development and progress of these nations, perpetuating poverty and inequality.

The social and cultural consequences of national borders in post-colonial Africa are also significant. Communities that were once connected and interdependent have been separated by borders, leading to the erosion of traditional social structures and cultural practices. This has resulted in a loss of cultural heritage and identity for many African ethnic groups.

Politically, European colonialism has had a lasting effect on ethnic groups in Africa. The imposition of colonial rule disrupted existing political systems and created power struggles among different ethnic groups. This has contributed to political instability and governance challenges that continue to plague many African countries to this day.

The environmental consequences of European colonialism and national borders in Africa are equally important to consider. The exploitation of natural resources by colonial powers has had devastating effects on the environment, leading to deforestation, land degradation, and loss of biodiversity. These environmental challenges continue to impact the livelihoods and well-being of ethnic groups in partitioned African countries.

The partitioning of ethnic groups and the imposition of colonial borders have also resulted in human rights issues and disparities in education and healthcare. Many ethnic populations have been marginalized and face discrimination and persecution. Educational disparities and healthcare challenges are prevalent in partitioned African countries, hindering the development and well-being of these communities.

Lastly, the migration patterns and displacement of ethnic populations as a result of colonial borders cannot be ignored. Many African nations continue to experience internal and cross-border migration due to the legacy of colonialism. This has led to further social, economic, and political complexities, exacerbating existing tensions and conflicts.

In conclusion, the ongoing legacy of European colonialism on African national borders is multifaceted and has far-reaching consequences. The effects of colonialism continue to shape the socio-political, economic, and cultural landscapes of African nations. As historians, it is crucial to acknowledge and understand these legacies to foster a deeper understanding of Africa's past and work towards a more equitable and inclusive future.

9 7 9 8 2 2 3 3 5 8 8 7 9